If you want to know how . . .

Hard Interview Questions Answered
The tough interview questions you're most likely to be asked – and inside information on how you should answer them

How to Succeed at Interviews
All you need to know to get the job you want

Get That Job!
The complete, thorough, hands-on guide to the whole recruitment and selection process – for ambitious graduates in early career

Management-Level Psychometric and Assessment Centre Tests

Passing Psychometric Tests

Practice Psychometric Tests

Psychometric Tests for Graduates

For full details, please send for a free copy
of the latest catalogue:

How To Books
Spring Hill House, Spring Hill Road, Begbroke
Oxford OX5 1RX, United Kingdom
info@howtobooks.co.uk
www.howtobooks.co.uk

Be prepared!

PASS
THAT JOB
INTERVIEW

REVISED and UPDATED
THIRD EDITION

JULIE-ANN AMOS

howtobooks

Published by How To Books Ltd,
Spring Hill House, Spring Hill Road, Begbroke,
Oxford OX5 1RX. United Kingdom.
Tel: (01865) 375794. Fax: (01865) 379162
info@howtobooks.co.uk
www.howtobooks.co.uk

How To Books greatly reduce the carbon footprint of their books
by sourcing their typesetting and printing in the UK.

First edition 2002
Second edition 2004
Third edition 2008

British Library Cataloguing in Publication Data.
A catalogue record for this book is available from the British Library.

ISBN 978 1 84528 267 7

Produced for How To Books by Deer Park Productions, Tavistock
Typeset by Kestrel Data, Exeter
Cover design by Baseline Arts Ltd, Oxford
Printed and bound by Cromwell Press Ltd, Trowbridge, Wiltshire

NOTE: The material contained in this book is set out in good faith for general
guidance and no liability can be accepted for loss or expense incurred as a
result of relying in particular circumstances on statements made in this book.
Laws and regulations are complex and liable to change, and readers should
check the current position with the relevant authorities before making
personal arrangements.

*We have attempted to acknowledge all known sources. We apologise for any that have
been missed. Please contact us so that we can include an acknowledgement in the next
edition.*

Contents

Preface

Job interviews can be daunting. This book will take you through the essentials of preparing for an interview. Whether it is your first interview, or your first in a long time – or even if you are an 'old hand' – you will find tips and hints for success.

Interviews can be some of the most stressful situations we have to face. From the moment you enter the potential employer's building to the time you are back outside, you are on show – and preparing to give a good performance is what can guarantee success or at least giving your best. You *can* tip the scales in your favour, with a little work beforehand.

Julie-Ann Amos

Chapter 1

Preparing for Interviews

Preparing for interviews starts before you even know you have an interview.

In this Chapter:

- **the purpose of interviews**
- **preparation**
- **getting your paperwork in order**
- **researching the company**
- **researching yourself**
- **getting from your front door to the interview.**

You can start your preparation before you even know you've been invited to an interview. Understanding the purpose of interviews, and being aware of the contents of your own curriculum vitae or application form is essential preparation for any interview.

You will need to assemble your job application paperwork carefully and put it in order so you can respond to short-notice invitations to attend interviews. Job hunting isn't easy and you may be surprised at the amount of organisation it takes.

For example, you may need to assemble facts and figures about your salary history and financial requirements, etc. Once invited to an interview, you will also need to assemble some information on the company that's interviewing you, but of course there's no point in preparing detailed information on companies until you know you've got an interview with them.

Is this you?

♦ Surely you can't prepare much for interviews, apart from getting basic information on the company that's going to interview you?

♦ Look, I know who I am and what jobs I've done. I don't need to memorise my own CV – I was there!

♦ I spend ages preparing and getting organised, but it's all wasted when I don't get an interview.

♦ I've sent off so many job applications that I can't remember who's who. It's all a bit of a mess, really.

The purpose of interviews

There's more than one type of interview – nowadays, interviews take many different forms (as we shall see) so that being aware of the different types of interview you may encounter can be very helpful. The How To book *Handling Tough Job Interviews*, also by Julie-Ann Amos, is very helpful in this regard but here are some of the main types.

Recruitment agency interviews

Recruitment agencies exist to place people in jobs. They make their money from the employer – the recruiter – and not from you. Therefore, the common assumption that recruitment agencies are there to help you may be something of a misconception.

Good agencies can be extremely helpful in looking after job hunters properly, by giving them help and support, and placing them in the right job. Others are purely serving the employment needs of the companies and organisations that pay their fees. They may be less concerned with meeting your own individual wants and needs, and more concerned with placing you in a job – any job – that will earn them a fee.

So recruitment agency interviews can be beneficial, as they will give you an opportunity to check out the agency and the way it operates. In an ideal world, the recruitment agency interview should be no more than a means of letting your agency know exactly what you want in a job – so it can tailor any applications it makes on your behalf specifically to your needs. Be aware of the way some agencies operate, however, and watch out for any attempt to 'sell you' a job that isn't in line with your requirements.

With a good agency, an interview can give you tips and advice on presenting yourself well, information on your strong and weaker points, and advice on how to conduct yourself in interviews with potential employers.

Employer interviews

Employer interviews are designed to allow the employer to assess whether or not you are a good fit with their requirements. Usually, a first interview is very much a screening interview, with a second interview being held later for those candidates who pass this initial screening. Your performance at the first interview should therefore really be a matter of being seen to be right for the job. Later interviews are where you would prove yourself to be the *best* candidate.

Personnel or Human Resources (HR) interviews

You will often encounter personnel or HR interviews, as most larger companies insist on them as part of the recruitment process. These interviews are sometimes viewed as 'easy', as HR interviewers rarely ask very technical questions about your specific skills – as they are HR specialists and not usually business managers. Questions are far more likely to revolve around other, more personal areas. But these interviews are not to be underestimated – HR specialists are often very highly trained and experienced in interviewing, and they usually carry out interviews on a regular basis. They are therefore skilled at getting information from you, so be careful – never attempt to pull the wool over their eyes.

> Not all interviews are alike – be aware of the purpose of an interview, and this will help you do well in all circumstances.

Preparation

Getting prepared is really what the whole of this book is about. So what exactly is it that you have to prepare? The first two chapters of the book focus on things you can *do* before the interview, and the rest of the book details information you can consider and think over before the interview as a means of preparing yourself for it.

Here are some examples of what you should prepare, ready for a round of potential interviews.

Paperwork
This includes your CV, a copy of the relevant application form, and all documents relating to a particular interview. Have copies of everything to hand well in advance – don't rely on technology (which can let you down) to print copies for you at the last minute.

Your 'shopping list'
Too many people attend interviews with no clear idea of exactly what they want and need from them. Make

sure you know what you do and don't want in terms of salary, environment, benefits, role etc.

Research

Make sure you have ready access to any research about the job, the company or organisation you have undertaken previously (see later). It may help you ask questions at interview or help you identify areas you need to clarify to see if this job opportunity meets your wants and needs list – your 'shopping list'.

What you will wear and take

All too often people leave these decisions until the last moment, rushing round looking for the right outfit on interview day. If you can, have your interview outfit cleaned in advance and ready to wear at short notice.

Transport

You need to research and plan the means of transport you intend to use to get to and from the interview. Thinking ahead will allow you to avoid running the risk of being late.

Things to think about

In addition, you will need to think about:

♦ how you will introduce yourself

♦ how to stay calm and relaxed, in what is for most people a stressful situation

♦ how to deal with the interviewer's questions

♦ preparing some sample answers to likely questions

◆ your body language, and how to establish a good rapport with your interviewer

◆ how to leave the interview gracefully and on a good note.

There are two stages to preparation – physically preparing, and mentally/academically thinking through the interview and potential difficulties you may encounter when you are interviewed.

Getting your paperwork in order

You need to make and have to hand copies of all your essential paperwork relating to the interviewer. You will need a copy of your CV, a copy of any job applications you send off, and the job adverts you are responding to. Of course, all this paperwork can be daunting and expensive to photocopy if you don't have access to a copier – and it can be hard to manage.

Be organised

Consider some sort of filing system. A cheap solution is a simple file or ring binder, in which you can collate job adverts and information by filing them, cutting out job adverts and sticking them onto A4 sheets of paper as necessary. This is important – if you get an interview, you need to be able to read up what you have available on the job and the company, and you need to check **exactly** what the employer is looking for, so you can tailor your thinking and preparation to giving a good performance for a particular job interview.

The filing system you use isn't important – what is important is that if anyone calls you to arrange an interview, you can find the information you need easily so you can prepare properly. You don't want to be getting stressed and anxious looking for the job advert in a pile of papers – you need to be calm and to prepare your thoughts carefully if you want to do well at the interview.

Job adverts

Job adverts usually give you a good idea of the skills and abilities the employer is looking for, so you need to read the job advert carefully if you are to prepare properly for an interview. If you are applying for a lot of jobs from adverts, you will need to be very organised, and to keep copies of all the adverts you reply to.

Application forms or packs

You will also need to consider application forms. If you have applied for jobs which involve filling out application forms, ideally you should keep a copy of the form you complete. You don't need to keep a copy of your basic details such as education, job history etc, as this is information that will be on your CV. But you do need to keep a copy of your answers to questions on the form such as 'Describe how you fit the job description', or 'Outline why you feel you are right for this role'. Your responses to questions like these may well be discussed at interview, so you really need to read through what you said on the form before going to the interview.

It's very useful that when an application form is sent to you, it will usually be part of a 'candidate pack', that will give you candidate information such as a job description, structure of the company department, etc. This is all good stuff that will help you to prepare for your interview. Again, it needs to be filed so you can find it when you need it – there's no worse way of preparing for an interview than having to conduct a last-minute paper chase!

You have a lot of resources available to help you prepare for interviews, but keeping them all organised and easily to hand can be almost as stressful as the interview itself!

Researching the company

Application or candidate packs

As mentioned above, when you get an application form, it will often be part of an application pack or candidate pack produced by the organisation. These packs can sometimes be very scrappy and hastily put together, but many of them are very well-presented and give you incredibly useful information about:

◆ what exactly the employer is looking for

◆ whether the employer's requirements are essential or desirable

- how the employer will test whether or not you fit a particular requirement

- special skills and abilities required by the employer

- information on working conditions at the workplace

- information about the organisation

- organisation charts setting out company/ departmental structures

- background to the department and/or the job

- details of salary and benefits, etc

- the recruitment process, and timescales relating to the process.

These packs can be the single most useful thing you have available to you for interview preparation, so keep them safe and read them carefully before the interview. They can help you understand how to present yourself in the best possible light, and give you ideas for questions to raise and points to clarify with the interviewer. Most importantly, they can give you a real feel for the job and the company they describe, which can be very useful in helping you decide whether or not the job is really for you.

If the company doesn't send you a pack, be proactive – call them and ask them for one. If you are invited to an interview, ask them to send you any information on the company they may have. Often companies send out a letter confirming an interview, and/or directions, so when they do, ask them to send you their company literature. If you don't ask, you don't get!

Other sources of company information

Even if you aren't sent an application pack, you can still obtain useful and relevant company information prior to your interview. You can research companies through media such as the internet, reference libraries and papers/journals, for example. Look for any material that will lead to increasing your knowledge of the company.

It is absolutely crucial you understand the culture and environment of the company by whom you will be interviewed, so that you can make the right decision as to whether you would be happy working for them. Research the organisation's history, its current market situation, clients, competitors etc.

The company website

Websites can give you a wealth of information about companies. If you don't know the address of a company's web site, look it up by using one of the major research engines such as Yahoo!, AltaVista, Google or Lycos.

Other internet websites

Here are some other good internet website sources of business information (correct at the time of printing).

www.prnewswire.co.uk
This is a European news network that covers press

releases and features. Allows searching for press releases by company name.

http://news.bbc.co.uk/hi/english/business/companies
This is the BBC news service that will give you all the latest news on companies.

www.thetimes.co.uk
You need to register to use this, but registration is currently free. There are selected news stories, from the latest editions of the two papers. You can search the archive back to January '96.

www.digitallook.com/dlmedia/news/company_news?
Another site with live company news feed, but not easy to search as with for example the BBC website above

Libraries
The reference section of your local library may have useful business directories such as Kompass, Dunn & Bradstreet and Kellys.

Papers/journals
Trade magazines are another useful source of company information.

Application packs are fantastic resources for interview preparation. Always ask for application packs where possible.

Researching yourself

Is this the job you really want?

As you have just read, application packs can help you decide whether or not a job is right for you. An essential part of your interview preparation should always be to evaluate your own needs, wants and desires. If you assess carefully how badly you want this particular job, you will approach the interview with the right mindset.

If you don't really feel the job is ideal for you, but that it's one you could settle for, you can approach the interview more as a means for giving you interview experience. But if the job is the one you really want – that elusive 'dream job' – then the interview becomes extremely important, and you will need to put all your effort into excelling at it.

Know your facts

You may be asked in detail at interview about your salary and benefits expectations. Make sure you know what they are as you may look rather foolish if you don't. Check out your hourly, weekly or monthly rate (however you are paid) and when you last had a pay rise. Know what benefits you get. If you don't know what you're paid at the moment, you will weaken your negotiating power.

Know what you want

Look at the job, and before you go into the interview decide the minimum salary or pay you would accept, should you be offered it. The job advert may list a salary or salary range, but a company may sometimes pay more for the right person, so always do your homework and decide on your minimum requirements.

When deciding your minimum requirements, you need to factor in additional costs. For example, if you will have a longer journey, your travelling expenses may be higher than you currently pay. Factor in extra costs like this to your requirements, so you can define:

♦ your ideal salary

♦ your minimum acceptable salary – your 'bottom line'.

It is absolutely essential that you know your absolute bottom line, so if you are offered a salary below this, you will know you need to decline the job offer.

Research salary requirements
Employers are very often open to a well-argued justification for a salary offer. If you have done your homework and are able to show it by justifying your salary requirements, they are much more likely to be met.

You can do this by looking at other adverts for similar jobs, or talking to people you know in similar jobs, etc. People who can produce evidence that they have researched their requirements are far more likely to get them accepted.

Take some credentials

Don't go overboard, but if it is appropriate take
to the interview some work you have done – drawings
you have done, or papers, reports you have written,
etc.

Research how badly you want the job, your
current position and needs, and your salary
requirements. Knowing the facts and doing the
necessary research will almost always pay
dividends.

Getting from your front door to the interview

One area you need to prepare in advance is how you
will actually get to the interview. You need to check
out, well in advance, both *how* you will get there –
bus, taxi, car, train – and *how long* this is likely to take.

Be on time

Being late for interviews isn't necessarily the end of
the world – a pleasant apology and good excuse can
prevent problems – but if an interviewer is working to
a schedule, you may end up not being able to have a
proper interview. Candidates turning up 30 minutes
late for a 45-minute interview place the interviewer in
a dilemma – do they give you a 30-minute interview
and 'steal' 15 minutes from their next candidate? That
isn't fair! Or do they only give you 15 minutes, which
more or less means you won't stand a chance! Don't
put them in that position – be on time.

Check schedules

Don't just plan to get a bus or train – actually check the departure and arrival times. Changes in schedule, repairs, etc can all stop scheduled services from running to plan. Check for last-minute updates, by using facilities such as train websites, AA Roadwatch on teletext, etc.

Be prepared for an emergency

Take a mobile phone, or change for the telephone with you – that way you can call ahead in an emergency, or if you are delayed.

Be generous

Be generous with your time. Delays, breakdowns, traffic, missed trains/buses, etc – all are reasonable, but at the same time avoidable excuses for being late. Allow sufficient time to get to the interview early, then find somewhere nearby to wait in comfort, so you can relax. Nothing makes people more stressed than a rushed journey, getting to the interview late or with seconds to spare. Plan to get there early and wait around – you can always use the time to prepare for your interview further, read through any notes, etc.

Plan your journey carefully, and allow extra time for unforeseen circumstances. Emergencies may be understandable, but getting there late can still mean you don't get a proper interview.

Summary points

♦ **Understand the purpose of interviews, so you can structure your preparation accordingly.**

♦ **Prepare all the necessary information – if you don't need to use it, at least you had it ready.**

♦ **Get all your paperwork ready – organise it so you can easily find the information you need.**

♦ **Research the company interviewing you so you can ask them sensible questions and resolve any queries you may have.**

♦ **Research your own wants and needs – and be prepared to justify them if necessary.**

♦ **Plan your journey with military precision, so everything goes smoothly on the day.**

Chapter 2

Presentation

Presentation is your window-dressing – the shop front you display to the world. A good display attracts more customers and makes them more likely to buy!

In this Chapter:

- **making a good impression**
- **what to wear**
- **personal presentation**
- **waiting.**

The best candidate can let themselves down and even lose a job at interview by being poorly presented. We all know it's wrong to judge by appearances, but let's face it, you also have to take human nature into account – people do. Before interviewing you, an interviewer will have made themselves look presentable, arranged a room, refreshments, read your CV, and prepared questions to ask you. In return, it is perfectly natural (and not unreasonable) for them to expect you to have made some effort yourself.

Presentation is all about appearances. A poor candidate can look good and make a decent impression by looking as though they have researched and prepared thoroughly for the interview, so impressions count.

But presentation is about more than just your appearance – anyone can make the effort to look good without buying new clothes. It's about letting the interviewer know you have tried – that you care about making a good impression, and that you take the interview seriously enough to prepare.

Is this you?

♦ People shouldn't judge by appearances. I should get the job based on what I can do, not what I look like.

♦ If I dress up for an interview, it looks too keen. I prefer to look as if I've just come from a normal day at work.

♦ Why bother? All the interviews I've had have been with people who didn't make any effort to look smart themselves!

♦ If I look too smart, everyone at work will know where I'm going – it's a bit of a give-away!

Making a good impression

Making a good impression isn't just about the clothes you wear. It's about the whole impression you give at interview. Everyone tends to focus on first impressions, and it's often said that interviewers decide within 30 seconds of meeting you whether or not they want you. Judgements are made on a conscious level within this short timeframe, it's true, and certainly we are all subconsciously influenced by first impressions to some extent.

So what goes into this impression? It's a mixture of factors, some of which you can influence, and some you can't:

♦ physical appearance

♦ dress

♦ manner – are you friendly, relaxed and approachable?

♦ what you say

♦ how you behave

♦ neatness

♦ timekeeping

♦ attitude – enthusiastic, shy, etc

♦ personal hygiene and grooming.

Most of these factors are subjective, not objective – that is, they cannot be measured, although some of them have at least some common standard. For example, although 'smart dress' is subjective, most people have a fairly clear idea of what they would agree is smart dress. Other factors such as physical appearance are very subjective indeed.

Given that, generally speaking, presentation is based on impressions that are subjective, just how can you prepare and make sure you present yourself well in all situations? You can't – not in all situations. You might turn yourself out spotlessly for interview to find that the company has a relaxed dress policy, for example, and everyone else is in jeans and shirts. What you can do is try your best to achieve a happy medium, so that you will do well in the majority of situations.

> Presentation is based on appearance, which is often in the eye of the beholder.

What to wear

Smart dress
What is meant by 'smart dress' is subjective. Be relatively conservative, and opt for something businesslike and appropriate to the situation – obviously some jobs or fields require different styles or standards of dress.

Pay attention to detail
Details such as odd or missing buttons, socks that don't match, torn clothing, frayed edges or loose ends all detract from your image. Check your clothes carefully before you put them on.

Colour

Choose a businesslike colour. Daffodil yellow may be your favourite colour, but a dark suit will probably go down better at interview. Splashes of colour, such as a colourful blouse or tie, can be stylish and they may make you more memorable and well-presented, but don't go too far. Save the more exotic components of your wardrobe for *after* you've got the job!

Shoes

Make sure that shoes are not scuffed or dirty, and that they go with the rest of your outfit. Beware of new shoes – it is easy to forget to remove those white labels from the bottom of your new shoes – not a serious mistake, but someone might see them and that's not what you want to be remembered for.

Personal comfort

Never underestimate personal comfort. Looking perfect at the price of your personal comfort rarely serves any purpose. Your discomfort may show without you realising it, especially in the case of shoes that pinch or rub. Wearing something comfortable will make you more relaxed and less stressed, and will allow you to behave more naturally.

> Deciding what to wear isn't actually that difficult. But don't leave things to chance – plan in advance and check all items carefully.

Personal presentation

Hygiene

There is more to presenting a good image than what
you wear. Interviews can often be in fairly small
rooms, so things like hygiene, body odour, bad breath,
etc, *will* be noticed.

Perfume/aftershave

Beware of wearing too strong a perfume or aftershave.
It can be overpowering in a small room, or it may be
not to the interviewer's liking. At the very least, it's
unnecessary. Wear something subtle, not strong.

Grooming

Basic details like having a hair cut if necessary,
washing your hair, clean fingernails, etc, shouldn't
need mentioning, but it's surprising how many
candidates forget to check these little details and turn
up for interviews with chipped nail polish, food on
their moustache, or hair that obviously hasn't been
brushed or combed! Do make sure you build in
enough time for a quick last minute check in the
mirror before your interview begins!

Shoes and bags

Shoes and bags are easily overlooked as well. Many
candidates dressed to perfection let themselves down
with old or scuffed shoes, or simply wear shoes that
obviously have no idea what polish is! Bags can also be
old and tired – and battered briefcases don't impress

anyone by looking well used; they just look scruffy.
Remember the details.

> There is more to how you look than your clothes.
> Your appearance can be enhanced by good dress,
> but no amount of smart dressing can cover up a
> basic hygiene or grooming problem.

Waiting

As we have said above, plan to get there early and
wait. Waiting can be more complex than you think,
however.

Where to wait

Bear in mind that there may be nowhere nearby to
wait. Not all businesses are conveniently situated near
shops and cafés, and you may have to wait at a location
ten or fifteen minutes' walk away if you want to wait
in a coffee bar or café. Or you could try waiting in
other places such as a local library. Ideally, you should
avoid waiting at the place of the interview. Try to
arrive early enough to find somewhere else to wait –
somewhere you can relax and feel calm and do some
last minute preparation if necessary.

Don't wait in a pub or bar – some people are sensitive
to cigarette smoke, and dislike it. Going into an
interview smelling of cigarette smoke may be
unpleasant for interviewers, particularly if the
interview takes place in a small room.

If you do have to wait at the place of the interview, for example if the weather is particularly bad, or the building is in a remote location or on an industrial estate, now is the time to be nice to the receptionist! Ideally, you want to be allowed to wait, but not be announced until the correct time. Interviewers may not be impressed by interviewees who are too early – it may create the impression that you are desperate to impress.

Ask the receptionist pleasantly if there is somewhere you can wait, but say that you would prefer not to be announced until at most five minutes before your interview time. When you are ready, don't forget to remind the receptionist that you are ready – you don't want to be forgotten and make the interviewer think you're late!

Eating and drinking whilst waiting

As we said above, many interview rooms can be quite small, and not everyone likes cigarette smoke. So, if you have a quick cigarette just before the interview to calm your nerves, have it in a well ventilated place and make sure your breath is fresh afterwards!

If you are having a coffee, tea or soft drink while you wait, beware of drinking too much – an interview can often last an hour, more if there is more than one person to see. You don't want to have to visit the loo halfway through! Coffee also contains chemicals that can add to your nervousness.

Beware of alcohol. A quick drink may be ideal for relaxing you or calming your nerves, but it may lead to over-confidence, and alcohol on the breath is rarely appreciated at any interview. The smell can also linger on your clothes, as with cigarettes.

Try to avoid either eating just before an interview, or being interviewed on an empty stomach. Either may cause embarrassment, particularly if your stomach starts to make noises during the interview.

Prepare to wait

Take with you your notes, a copy of the job advert, and any other relevant literature you have and have a last-minute read through everything, so it is fresh in your mind.

Arriving early only to hang about is pointless. Plan to use waiting time to maximum effectiveness. Being busy while you wait will reduce your stress levels.

Summary points

♦ **Making a good impression is about more than the way you look.**

♦ **Choose your interview clothes and accessories carefully. It's not a fashion parade – it's about creating the right image and impression.**

- Don't ignore your personal presentation.

- Plan your journey to the interview with military precision, allowing for contingencies and waiting time.

- Hanging about isn't waiting. Waiting is a slot of time you can use effectively to calm and prepare yourself.

Chapter 3

Meeting and Greeting

First impressions count – there's no denying it. They can also be changed and influenced.

In this Chapter:

- **arriving**
- **breaking the ice**
- **shaking hands**
- **accepting refreshments**
- **sitting down.**

There is a common saying that an interviewer decides within the first 30 seconds of meeting you whether or not he/she wants to hire you. This is unlikely to be true, especially now that managers are becoming more and more enlightened, more aware of 'human factors' such as psychology, and are better trained in interviewing techniques, etc.

However, there is no denying the fact that preconceptions and prejudices exist, as do instant reactions. People do tend to react positively or negatively to others quite quickly; to get around this at interview you have to bear in mind that you *can* influence interviewers, even to the extent of changing an initial negative reaction. Obviously, the quicker you start to influence them, the better, so the early stages of an interview are vital, when you are introducing yourself, meeting and greeting, etc.

Some people make their minds up less quickly, and are initially objective, forming their opinion of you over a longer period of time. Again, influencing them early on helps them to make the right decision about you.

Is this you?

♦ I hate it when you can see that people have prejudged you. It's not fair!

♦ This is a big deal for just getting into a room with someone – it seems over-complicated.

♦ The beginning is just when I'm *most* nervous. I don't need all these extra things to worry about.

♦ The whole meeting and greeting thing is a con trick. Let's face it, they're just trying to lull you into a false sense of security for the grilling that's to come.

Arriving

From the moment you enter . . .
You're on show right from the start:

- You may be on security camera from the moment you enter the building

- Receptionists/PAs, etc, may be asked their opinion, or what they thought of you, so be on your best behaviour with everybody from the moment you step into the building.

Remember what people look for

- People like people who are like themselves

- People like people who can initiate conversation if necessary

- People like others to respond if they initiate conversation

- People like people with confidence (but not too much!)

- People relate to people who can express themselves appropriately

Bags, coats and other baggage

- Try to avoid carrying too much baggage

- Ladies should avoid carrying both a handbag and briefcase – it's too much

- If possible, avoid carrying multiple items such as a coat and umbrella *and* briefcase into the interview

- Ask if you can leave things in reception before you are announced – it shows confidence as well as getting rid of the clutter!

- Discard or put away newspapers, etc before arriving

- If you have a file of interview information, by all means carry it so they will know you have gone to the time and trouble of preparing, but don't be too obvious about it – understated is best.

> Arriving is important – it's part of those vital first few seconds.

Breaking the ice

Start the ball rolling

Never be afraid to initiate conversation if necessary. It shows confidence without being pushy. Safe comments are things like 'It's a beautiful day, isn't it?' or 'What a lovely building; have you been here long?'

Respond appropriately

If a conversation is started, don't rush in too quickly. 'Small talk' is an appropriate phrase – most interviewers start off with a few quick and easy questions and comments to get people relaxed and comfortable. So don't give a great long explanation to a question at this stage. Keep your answers short, to the point, and positive.

Beware of negatives

Even if you have had the journey from hell to get to your interview, play things down if asked about it. Starting off on a negative footing isn't really ideal. It may not do you any harm, but it is unlikely to do you any good either. Journey and travel details are often a potential pitfall. Remember, if you get the job they will be expecting you to travel to work every day, on time. So giving the information that the journey was long or difficult isn't giving them the impression it would be easy for you to work for them! If you need to explain lateness, for example, end with a positive note, such as 'The journey coming from my current place of work was a nightmare – obviously coming here from home would be much easier.'

Body language

With body language, three things seem to make people relate to each other quickly and easily at a first meeting:

- Make eye contact – look them in the eye

- Smile – to show you are pleased to see them

- The 'eyebrow flash' – quickly raising your eyebrows when being introduced apparently shows interest in the other person and indicates a willingness to establish a good relationship.

The first few seconds of being introduced are actually a good opportunity to get things off on the right foot.

Shaking hands

Don't panic!

People very often dread shaking hands, and yet it's a minor thing that is usually over in a second or two. It's hard to see why people are so nervous about it. It does, however, give an important element to the impression you make in those vital first few minutes.

Sweaty palms

You may have sweaty palms. At worst, this can be obvious and unpleasant. On the other hand, it may not even be consciously noticed by the interviewer, but subconsciously you could be transmitting a signal that you are nervous. Very discreetly and without being noticed, wipe your hand before shaking your interviewer's hand. For example, you could rest your right hand on your leg when waiting, and as you stand up or step forward to shake, just run your palm over your clothes. Never be seen to wipe your hand before shaking – it shows you feel dirty and unworthy to touch them – it's very subordinate. Conversely, *never* wipe your hand after shaking someone else's – it shows you didn't like touching the other person!

The 'dead fish'

A limp handshake is sometimes known as the 'dead fish'. We've all at sometime shaken someone's hand and it's been floppy and lifeless. Feels awful, doesn't it? Don't fall into this trap yourself – hold your interviewer's hand firmly. Limp handshakes come across as unconfident. This type of handshake says:

- I'm not confident

- I don't have any character

- I'm not comfortable shaking hands

- I'm nervous.

The 'death grip'

On the other hand, don't grip someone's hand too strongly. People resent it, and it has become something of a stereotype, and may be seen as the action of an aggressive business person. It's true that some employers *want* a firm handshake, especially for sales-type roles, if they're looking for a strong character. But tread carefully – be guided by your interviewer. If your interviewer gives you a 'death grip', responding in kind will probably be the right thing to do. Too-firm handshakes, however, are definitely inappropriate for older (ie, elderly) interviewers, and some ladies – they can hurt. And if you are shaking hands with someone who's your equal, it becomes a competitive gesture. Be sensible about how strong your handshake grip is – the 'death grip' handshake says:

- I'm overconfident

- I'm competitive

- I'm insensitive

- I'm pushy

- I'm trying to dominate

- I'm trying to force my ideas

- I'm trying to give you a message.

The perfect handshake

- Engage the whole hand, palm to palm.

- Match the hand pressure of the other person. If they are a person with a firm handshake, you want to shake back just as firmly. For people with a weaker handshake you should soften your handshake grip in return.

- It shouldn't last longer than how long it takes to say 'One, two, three.'

- Accompany the handshake with a smile and eye contact.

> Shaking hands takes no more than a second or two, but it all adds to the interviewer's impression of you.

Accepting refreshments

The golden rule

The golden rule is to be comfortable, so that you can relax. So if you are desperately thirsty, of course you should accept refreshments.

Extreme nerves

If you are so nervous you fear spilling something, politely say 'No, thank you' and decline. Better to do this than to accept in an attempt to co-operate with the interviewer and then have a catastrophe!

Check what your interviewer does

By far the safest option is to ask if the interviewer is having anything. Some people feel embarrassed if they are offered coffee and accept, and then the interviewer doesn't join them. Say something simple such as:

♦ 'I'll join you if you're having something, otherwise I'm fine, thank you.'

♦ 'Only if you're going to.'

♦ 'Are you having anything?'

Smoking and eating

Never ever smoke or eat in an interview, regardless of what the interviewer does. Interviews are about answering the interviewer's questions, and it's hard to talk when you are eating or smoking. You end up juggling words and mouthfuls, and it just looks clumsy.

> You can see what a disaster area refreshments can be – be careful before accepting.

Sitting down

Wait your turn!

Never sit down before being invited to do so. Waiting is not only polite, it gives a nervous interviewer confidence, and gives them the lead.

Be alert and interested

The aim in an interview is to appear alert and interested. You can't do this if you are slumped. Lean slightly forward – not too much or you will look odd! Sit up straight.

Stay relaxed

Stay relaxed but not slumped. Sitting uncomfortably and bolt upright may look great at first, but after 30 minutes it may be so uncomfortable that your whole body language changes – the interviewer isn't a mindreader and he/she may decide you aren't happy with the job or the company if you *look* unhappy.

Do something with your hands

Oddly enough, when sitting down, one of the hardest things to do is to decide what to do with your hands! Don't dangle them off the arms of the chair – it's odd. And don't clutch them together, which looks nervous. Find a relaxed way of holding them or laying them on your legs.

Territory and positioning

You may get to choose where to sit, or the interviewer may direct you to a seat. This positioning is rarely random – so choose your territory carefully. Don't sit facing a bright light, or with the sun in your eyes. If possible don't sit directly opposite the interviewer face-to-face, looking directly at each other – it's confrontational and may make some interviewers feel uncomfortable. Try to sit at an angle to them if at all possible. You can easily do this by moving your chair very slightly as you sit down, so you are positioned at a slight angle to them.

Avoid closed body language

Avoid folding your arms and crossing your legs – closing your body language. It says you are unreceptive and not willing to listen.

> How you sit says a lot to the interviewer, and subconsciously it will be adding to their opinion of you.

Summary points

♦ **Remember you may be noticed from the second you enter the building.**

♦ **Breaking the ice may be something you have to initiate.**

♦ **Shaking hands appropriately takes only a few seconds but adds to the image you are presenting.**

♦ Accept refreshments where necessary and/or appropriate.

♦ Even something as simple as the way in which you sit down can convey a message to the interviewer.

Chapter 4

Handling Nerves

Being nervous isn't just a rotten feeling to have to experience – it can ruin your chances of giving your best performance as well!

In this Chapter:

♦ **handling emotions**
♦ **transforming thought processes**
♦ **relaxing and calming yourself**
♦ **emergency measures.**

Being nervous can be a pretty unpleasant feeling. Nobody likes to feel anxious, under-confident, fearful of the situation, unsure of themselves – and most people have experienced one or more of these feelings at some time or other.

But the risk of feeling bad isn't the only problem. Uncontrolled nervousness can alter your behaviour, your body language and what you say – when you feel nervous you can behave differently to how you usually behave. And interviews are doubly difficult because both you and the interviewer may be nervous.

Controlling your nerves isn't easy, and even if it were, it's one more thing to have to think about in what is an inherently stressful situation. But keeping your anxiousness under control can reap such huge benefits that it is certainly worthwhile. And nerves *can* be controlled. Learning simple techniques will at first help, and eventually may even become an unconscious habit, so you automatically control your nerves better.

Is this you?

♦ I hate interviews. I never do well, and I never will. What's the point?

♦ I don't believe you can ever really control nerves – some people are just more nervous than others and that's that.

♦ It's all right for interviewers – they don't get nervous.

♦ If I spend all my time controlling my nerves, how will I be able to concentrate on the interview itself and on doing myself justice?

Handling emotions

Thoughts versus emotions

With nerves, is it really your emotions that are a problem? In many ways, the problem is more often a thought process than an actual emotion. Let me explain. Thoughts and emotions are not the same. For example:

THOUGHT	EMOTION GENERATED
'This is a scary situation'	Fear
'I might not get the job'	Nervousness or anxiety
'Damn, I messed that up!'	Hopelessness
'I should have said X instead . . .'	Frustration

Controlling emotions

As you can see, it is actually thoughts that generate emotions. Someone who feels fear, anxiety, nervousness, hopelessness, frustration, etc, would find it very difficult to do anything about it – and that's perfectly natural. But just how do you *stop* being afraid?

The problem is that once the emotion is there, it's happening, and very hard to stop. Often these emotions produce complex hormonal or chemical reactions in the body, and controlling reactions is next to impossible. The key to controlling any emotion – such as nervousness, for example – is to remember that it is caused by a thought process. Disrupt the thought process and you cut off the stimulus that causes the emotion.

Thoughts and emotions are not the same at all.
You can influence your thoughts, but your
emotions are a reaction to them.

Transforming thought processes

Internal dialogue

For nervousness, you need to identify the thought
process behind your nervousness and so deal with it
more positively. You do this by internal dialogue.
Discuss the thought process with yourself, and try just
focusing on the thoughts – that will take your
attention away from the emotion and its biological
effects on your system. Don't worry that you won't
have time for this – conducting internal dialogue is
pretty quick for most people; these split-second
'conversations' usually go on in our heads all the time.

Identify thought processes

♦ Identify the thought process, eg, 'I might not get
   the job.'

♦ Doing this takes your mind off the emotion you are
   feeling.

♦ It also refocuses your attention.

Evaluate rationally

♦ Evaluate the thought *rationally* – this means
   examining it unemotionally.

- Is it justified to that extent?

- Is it even true?

- Would the consequences that you fear really be all that bad?

- Talk it over with yourself – *rationally*, eg, 'They wouldn't have interviewed me if they didn't think I was a possibility. If I don't get it, there are other jobs out there. But I might get it – who knows?'

Replace the negative thought with something more helpful

- amend it

- replace with a more sensible, appropriate and/or positive thought, eg, 'I might get the job or I might not. Either way this is valuable experience I can learn from.'

Re-examine how you feel

- Re-examine the emotion you feel

- It should either be reducing or gone, eg, 'Hey! If I see it as a learning experience, this interview doesn't make me feel quite so nervous!'

Amending the thought processes behind emotions helps us to control unwanted emotions such as nervousness.

Relaxing and calming yourself

Breathe

♦ Getting oxygen to your brain will make you able to think more clearly.

♦ Breathe deeply and slowly.

♦ Try breathing in for a count of five, then out for a count of five.

♦ Get some fresh air. Like breathing, this will increase the supply of oxygen to your brain and make you able to think more clearly.

♦ Take a short walk – for the same reason.

Calming rituals

♦ People often have calming rituals, such as having a cigarette or a cup of tea. If you don't have one, establish one!

♦ Have a drink – preferably a soft drink, juice or water.

♦ Remember that tea and coffee are stimulants, so if you are very nervous, they won't help and could even make things worse – caffeine can make you feel even more anxious!

Relaxing yourself

♦ Find somewhere to sit down.

♦ Concentrate on relaxing.

- Starting with your feet and moving up, tighten each part of your body in turn and then relax it. This will remove any muscle tension.

- Concentrate on relaxing your body – stop nervous, edgy movements and actions such as fiddling, licking your lips, biting lips, tapping feet, etc.

> Relaxing and calming yourself is something you need to do physically. Just the act of physically concentrating on changing things helps your mind focus on something constructive and positive, and will reduce nervousness.

Emergency measures

Keep things in proportion

- You are not alone. Everyone dries up at some stage.

- Sometimes the physical effects of anxiety can affect the vocal chords and make it hard to speak. Or you get so nervous you don't know *what* to say.

- Panicking will only make things worse.

Buy yourself some time

- Ask for a glass of water.

- Not only will the water help, but the time it takes to get it for you will buy you some breathing space so you can collect your thoughts.

◆ Use this to try to relax.

◆ Pause in your conversation, or when asked a question. Count to five then continue. This doesn't sound as odd as you might think – pausing to gather your thoughts is a natural thing, and people often do it.

◆ Ask for thinking time. You can always say 'Can I have a minute to think this one through?'

◆ If you're asked a difficult question, ask if you can come back to it. It's not ideal, but can be acceptable. For example, you might say, 'Sorry, can we come back to that question?'

Refocus on something else

◆ Stop thinking about being nervous, and start thinking about relaxing.

◆ Refocus your attention – use some of the internal dialogue technique we have previously discussed.

Come clean and ask for help

◆ Admit it! Admitting honestly to being nervous can help the interviewer carry out the interview. There is nothing wrong with saying honestly (but not in a grovelling way) something such as 'I'm sorry – I'm actually quite nervous about this interview, as I really like the look of this job.' Giving a positive reason for your nervousness will make you seem less like a shrinking violet.

Everyone gets nervous at times. Being able to control this and turn it to your advantage, can help your performance greatly, as well as making you feel a whole lot better!

Summary points

♦ Learn that emotions can be handled – they aren't something that you are totally at the mercy of, something you can only suffer until they go away.

♦ The key to handling emotions is to identify and amend the thought processes that underlie them. This is done by internal dialogue.

♦ Learn physical mechanisms that help to relax and calm you – and use them.

♦ Remember that you can cope with an emergency, by resorting to emergency measures.

Chapter 5

Body Language

Body language is a huge subject. Understanding it can make life a lot easier, as it can add greatly to the image you present to an interviewer.

In this Chapter:

- **the golden rule**
- **gestures and meanings**
- **eye contact**
- **listening skills**
- **mirroring**
- **disagreeing.**

Body language is a huge subject upon which many books have been written. Unfortunately, they can sometimes give you conflicting advice, while studying body language in depth can mean you spend all your time studying other people's mannerisms instead of concentrating on your own! You need to have enough information to allow you to focus on performing at your best at interview. Knowing the basics of body language can increase your performance at interview greatly. Being able to control your own body language makes it easier for you to relate to interviewers, and to make a good impression. It can also make you appear

more confident, more honest, and more in tune with
the interviewer.

But there is one other advantage of knowing about
body language – it helps you control your nerves,
if you suffer from nervousness. Concentrating on
your physical actions will take your attention
away from negative thought processes and feeling
nervous, and make you focus instead on what you are
actually doing. This can reduce your nervousness
significantly.

Is this you?

♦ I can't be bothered with body language – I
   already have a million things to think about in
   an interview!

♦ Everyone knows about body language now so
   it's irrelevant. We all know what things mean,
   so there's no big secret advantage to knowing
   it any more.

♦ I think all the advice I've ever seen on body
   language is just false – it just makes people
   look silly, as if they're acting.

♦ I know the basics and what not to do – but can
   you really use body language to make an
   interviewer like you more?

The golden rule

The golden rule with body language is to match your interviewer's body language. Like attracts like.

Match verbal with non-verbal behaviours

♦ Use non-verbal behaviour – ie, body language, to reinforce and back up what you are saying verbally.

♦ Try never to use body language that gives a different message from your verbal message, such as saying 'Yes' and shaking your head at the same time, or a more common example, saying 'No' and nodding.

♦ The trick is to always match non-verbal messages with verbal messages – so you should always nod when you agree, shake your head when you are disagreeing, etc.

Mismatching

So what happens if you mismatch – if you literally do say 'yes' and at the same time shake your head? (Try it – it's actually quite hard to do!) Research varies, but almost every piece of research that has been carried out on the subject shows that the *non-verbal* signal will come through strongest. So the non-verbal signal will be the one believed, and the other person may reject the content of your words, or they will not even notice the words at all, but will end up feeling you've said what your non-verbal signal said!

Other types of matching

There are other ways in which you can use the principle of matching, that like attracts like. These will be explained later, but in particular, a technique called 'mirroring', is useful. This is where you match, or mirror, the other person's body language, which almost always has the effect of making the person you're talking to feel more in rapport with you – they relate to you better.

> Like attracts like. People like people like them. People relate better to people they feel 'in synch' with. This is one of the fundamental aspects of body language.

Gestures and meanings

As we have said, an amazing number of books on body language have been published. Listing the things you can do to convey certain meanings isn't always helpful, as it will give you too much to think about in a situation which we know is inherently stressful.

Instead, here are some of the main impressions you may give to an interviewer, and some of the main signals by which your body language conveys these impressions. Choose which ones to practise and which ones to avoid – that way, you can focus on improving just one area at a time, which won't overload you!

Defensiveness

These actions convey the impression that you have something to hide:

♦ crossing or folding your arms

♦ sitting at too much of an angle to the interviewer, so you have to turn your head to look at him/her

♦ pointing your finger when making a point

♦ using your hand in a 'karate chop' gesture when making a point

♦ looking down when speaking

♦ not making eye contact.

Suspicious and distrusting

These actions suggest you are distrusting:

♦ crossing or folding your arms

♦ looking at your interviewer from underneath your eyebrows

♦ looking at your interviewer sideways – out of the corner of your eye (usually caused by sitting too much at an angle to him/her)

♦ rubbing your eyes

♦ frowning

♦ touching nose or face

♦ rubbing the back of the neck

Nervousness

All these convey nervousness:

♦ pinching your skin

♦ fidgeting

♦ jiggling the contents of your pockets

♦ running your tongue along the front of your teeth

♦ clearing your throat

♦ running your fingers through your hair

♦ wringing your hands

♦ biting on pens or other objects

♦ twiddling your thumbs

♦ biting your fingernails (both the action itself and evidence of it)

♦ tongue-clicking

♦ gritting your teeth

♦ biting your lips

Positive body language

All these actions, on the other hand, will enable you to establish a good rapport with interviewer:

♦ good eye contact

♦ leaning forward slightly in your chair

- tilting your head whilst maintaining eye contact with your interviewer

- open-lipped smiling

- open hands with palms visible

- unbuttoning your coat or jacket upon being seated

- keeping your chin up

- putting tips of fingers of one hand against the tips of fingers of other hand in the 'praying' or 'steepling' position

- having your hands joined behind back your when standing.

Body language can be a lot to take in and master. Concentrate on identifying the bad habits and eliminating them, and add a few good ones.

Eye contact

The importance of eye contact

- Eye contact is important as it conveys confidence and trust.

- It establishes a rapport with the other person – ie, a link, a connection or relationship between you.

♦ When speaking to someone, establishing eye contact allows you to check that they understand and are still interested in what you are saying.

♦ When listening, establishing eye contact conveys your attention and is a gesture of politeness.

♦ Lack of eye contact shows evasiveness, and makes it almost impossible to establish rapport with someone.

Eye contact when listening

There are two ways of looking at eye contact – either as a listener or as a speaker. As a listener, you need to make a great deal more eye contact – it's simply more appropriate for a listener to do so, and to extend your eye contact for longer periods of time than if you are speaking.

Eye contact when speaking

On the other hand, if you are a speaker, your listener will end up feeling uncomfortable if you maintain complete eye contact with them for too long. About five to ten seconds of eye contact is about right for making a connection with your listener. After that you should make your eye contact less complete. Otherwise, the connection with your listener becomes too intense, and can start to feel like a staring match. Speakers tend therefore to make and break eye contact regularly, whereas listeners tend to keep eye contact for extended periods of time.

Excessive eye contact

Excessive or inappropriate eye contact will prevent you from establishing a good rapport with your interviewer:

♦ eye contact that is too strong can be too intense

♦ it can become a battle of wills

♦ it can be intimidating

♦ it can be over-familiar

♦ holding eye contact for too long can make people uncomfortable

♦ it can make you look stupid as a listener (as if you are a zombie drinking in every word!)

♦ glancing away occasionally is perfectly acceptable, so long as you restore contact quickly.

Eye contact is probably the most important element of body language. It can make or break the rapport between people in a very short time.

Listening skills

Active listening

Listening isn't just something you do with your ears! It is something you have to do actively in an interview – you don't just have to listen, you have to be *seen* to be listening. This is active listening. Listening signals or behaviours include:

- making eye contact

- nodding

- making 'listening noises' ('Mmm', 'Uh-huh', etc)

- smiling

- leaning forward

- open body language

- tilting the head to one side

- reacting to what your interviewer is saying.

Concentration

The easiest way to listen properly is purely and simply to concentrate on what the person is saying! This tends to make most people exhibit at least some of the signs of active listening listed above.

Questioning

There are other, non-body language ways you can enhance your listening skills. A good way of either showing you have been listening or checking your understanding is to ask questions. You don't necessarily need to interrupt – wait until they pause or stop, and then off you go; it's your turn. Try 'Can I just check I got that correctly . . . ?'

Reflecting

Reflecting is repeating back what you just heard, in a way that isn't obvious. It checks your understanding is correct, and also shows them you understood. It also means that you are telling them what they just told you – and remember that people like people who are like them – it will add to the matching effect you are trying to create. Here are some reflecting phrases:

♦ 'So what you're saying is . . . ?'

♦ 'So you think . . . ?'

♦ 'Then would you agree that . . . ?'

♦ I agree. It *is* important that . . .'.

Listening is an active, not passive process. It is a good opportunity to relax and make a good impression at the same time.

Mirroring

What is mirroring?

Mirroring is when you imitate someone else's body language. It is like reflecting, except that reflecting is a means of establishing a rapport with someone verbally, whereas mirroring is its non-verbal equivalent. It is basically copying someone else's body language.

Why mirror?

♦ people like people like themselves

♦ it helps you establish a rapport with your interviewer

- it establishes a connection between you and your interviewer

- it strengthens any connection or rapport between you that may already exist

A word of caution

Mirroring is something that many books on body language refer to. But many attempts at mirroring go badly wrong, as this is a very subtle technique. You need to mirror very carefully and gently, so it isn't at all obvious, otherwise you will look very strange indeed! Remember:

- never mirror aggressive interviewers

- don't mirror nervous people

- don't mirror bad habits like scratching

- only mirror people who themselves have good body language

- don't overdo it! – be very, very, subtle

- if you make it obvious that you are mirroring, you have failed.

Mirroring gestures

Mirroring *gestures* is where many people go wrong – it's simply too obvious. If someone smiles, smiling back is mirroring, but it also looks perfectly natural. But crossing your legs as soon as the other person does can look ludicrous.

- Don't mirror immediately – leave a gap of a few seconds.

- Don't mirror exactly – you could mirror crossed legs by crossing your ankles, for example.

- Be subtle – mirror reduced versions of what your interviewer is doing; For example, you could mirror their running a hand through their hair by just brushing back your fringe or tucking your hair behind one ear.

- Remember you don't have to produce an exact mirror image – if your interviewer leans to the left, wait a short while then lean either to the left or right yourself – it is the leaning you are mirroring, not its precise direction.

Mirroring is very effective for establishing rapport and contact with the interviewer. Unfortunately, it is very hard to do subtly, and many people end up looking foolish.

Disagreeing

Your right to an opinion

Interviewers are in charge during an interview situation, and it's true that they do control whether or not you get the job. But that doesn't mean you have to agree with everything they say – it might curry favour, but it may be against what you really believe, and may even make you look weak.

Tell the truth, and if you disagree with something the interviewer says, don't be afraid to say so – nicely! Most people would rather someone stood up for themselves than agreed with everything. Plus, there is always the chance that the interviewer is merely testing you – saying something they *expect* you to disagree with, to see whether or not you have the strength of character to do so.

You may also find that if you agree with them because you think it will look better, later on – in the interview or afterwards – it becomes apparent that you have been 'found out'. It's far better never to be dishonest, and so there *will* be occasions when you need to be true to yourself and disagree with an interviewer.

Question before disagreeing

If you disagree with something your interviewer says, check your understanding first. Ask a question or questions to clarify his/her meaning, before saying you disagree. It is far better to make sure you didn't misunderstand before you put your cards on the table.

Be surprised to disagree

Obviously, some people are concerned about disagreeing with an interviewer, as they don't want to give a bad impression. A good way to counteract this is to show surprise when you disagree – as if you expected to agree with the other person, thus creating an impression of how similar you are – good old matching again! Say you're surprised, and use body language to reinforce what you are saying, by raising your eyebrows and saying, for example:

- 'Well, I've always been in favour of . . . myself.'

- 'I'm surprised – I actually don't find that myself.'

- 'How strange – I found them/it very helpful.'

- 'That's interesting, because I haven't found that to be the case.'

Don't lie

Don't fall into the trap of lying and agreeing for the sake of it. If you get found out, you will have shown yourself to be dishonest, and that is one thing interviewers hate!

Disagree graciously

One reason why people don't want to disagree with things that are said to them in interviews is because they don't want to be confrontational. Disagree politely and graciously, and there should be no problem. Apologising for disagreeing (without grovelling!) is easy and doesn't seem too submissive:

'I'm sorry, I don't agree. I've always thought that . . .'

Disagreeing isn't always a complete 'no-no' with interviewers. Better to stand up for yourself and disagree without confrontation than to be caught out in a lie later.

Summary points

♦ Remember the golden rule – people like people like themselves. Matching where possible to establish common ground and rapport is your aim.

♦ Beware of using negative body language and try to make a positive impression on your interviewer by using positive body language.

♦ Eye contact is absolutely critical. But don't overdo it, and make sure you use listening or speaking eye contact as appropriate.

♦ Listening needs to be an active process, so don't just sit there – You need to be seen to be listening!

♦ Mirroring is something that is hard to do properly. Leave well alone unless you are confident in your ability to do it well.

♦ Disagreeing with your interviewer is fine so long as you do it appropriately, and aren't in any way confrontational or aggresive.

Chapter 6

Answering Questions

People get very hung up about being questioned at interview. It's not actually the biggest problem you'll have to tackle in your interview, and let's face it, you should know the answers if you are being asked about yourself!

In this Chapter:

- **understanding good questions**
- **dealing with bad questions**
- **correcting mistakes**
- **reinforcing your message.**

Being questioned about your CV, your skills and experience is the real core of an interview. Only by doing this can the interviewer establish whether or not you are a good fit with the requirements of the position for which you are being interviewed.

So everyone attending an interview expects to be questioned. Perhaps that is why answering questions gets blown up out of all proportion in many people's minds, and why they get so worked up about finding good answers to them.

The bulk of questions in any interview will be about you – what you've done, how you think and behave, what you think and feel. There is no reason why anyone should worry about answering this sort of question, as you know yourself (and therefore the answers) better than anybody! But what concerns everyone is how to present those answers in the best possible light – how to make yourself look really good at interview. Understanding questions and answers can help here.

Is this you?

♦ I hate interviews. I just feel like I'm being interrogated, no matter how nice they are.

♦ I know my own life, but I just panic when the questions start – some people word them so awkwardly I can't tell what they really want me to say!

♦ Anyone can answer a simple question – it's getting it just right so I look better than the others that counts.

♦ If the interviewers knew how to ask questions better it would be easier! Half the time I can't answer the question, because it isn't what they actually want to know . . . .

Understanding good questions

The aim of an interviewer is to get you to tell them

what they need to know, in order to make their decision. They need to get you to talk, so they can listen and pick out the information they need. So the aim of any question isn't necessarily to 'catch you out', it's to get you to talk to them!

Good questions

There are three main types of 'good questions':

♦ open questions

♦ probing questions

♦ forced choice questions.

Open questions

These are questions with no set answer, which force you to talk freely. For example:

♦ 'Tell me about your time at . . .'

♦ 'Talk me through your last three jobs.'

♦ 'Tell me a little bit more about . . .'

♦ 'What do you think you gained from that?'

Probing questions

These are questions which force you to go into a little more detail. They require less of an answer, but a more specific answer. Probing questions tend to use the words:

♦ 'Who . . . ?'

- 'What . . . ?'

- 'Where . . . ?'

- 'When . . . ?'

- 'How . . . ?'

- 'Why . . . ?'

Forced choice questions

Forced choice questions are designed to put you on the spot. They force you to make a choice of answer. As questions they are actually not as good as the other two types, as they can often be answered with one or two words, or even a 'Yes' or 'No', which doesn't really encourage you to talk. For this reason they are usually followed up with a probing question, such as 'Why?' or 'Could you explain that?' Here are some examples of forced choice questions:

- 'Did you enjoy that type of work or not?'

- 'Do you prefer tasks in stages or whole projects to get on with?'

- 'Are you very organised or more spontaneous?'

- 'Do you get more satisfaction from team work or achieving something alone?'

Good questions are designed to make you talk, so try to give full answers, not just a couple of words. Explain without being asked to – it helps the interviewer.

Dealing with bad questions

Bad questions are questions that close you down, and
make it easy for you to say very little. They are also
questions that don't actually give the interviewer any
useful information about you or your suitability for the
job. Good interviewers don't ask bad questions, but
here are some of the types of bad questions you may be
asked at interview.

Closed questions

Closed questions are poor because they only require a
very short or simple 'Yes' or 'No' answer. They 'close
you down' and either prevent you from saying very
much, or let weak candidates get away without
elaborating their answers. Here are some examples:

♦ 'Did you like working there?'

♦ 'How many staff did you have?'

♦ 'Were you there long?'

If you are asked a closed question, deal with it by
answering in a reasonable amount of depth anyway –
as if the interviewer had asked you to expand your
answers.

Leading questions

Leading questions are questions that tell you exactly
what answer the interviewer wants you to give. Asking
leading questions is bad because it enables weak
candidates to get away with doing fairly well at
interview – as they can guess what the interviewer

wants them to say! It's also bad for strong candidates, as it makes it hard for them to disagree with the interviewer without knowing that this will be unexpected and unwelcome. Here are some examples of leading questions:

♦ 'So you liked it there?'

♦ 'I've always thought X, don't you agree?'

♦ 'I assume you left because . . .'

♦ 'That was a pretty senior role, wasn't it?'

Deal with leading questions by standing up for yourself. Try the 'Yes, but . . .' approach – it could work well for you.

Multiple questions
Multiple questions are where the interviewer asks several questions at once. They are bad questions because they confuse candidates, and make it hard for them to create a good impression by giving the interviewer the information he/she wants. Here are some examples of multiple questions:

♦ 'Did you like working there? They're fairly laid back, aren't they?'

♦ 'What would you choose, why would that particularly be your first choice, and do you foresee any particular problems?'

♦ 'Why did you leave there – I imagine it must have been a wrench – didn't you work there for quite some time?'

Deal with multiple questions by answering all parts of the question if possible. Organise your thoughts by numbering the questions, for example: 'Firstly, I didn't, and secondly, that was because . . .'. It will help you remember to answer all the questions within the question. If you lose track, just ask politely for them to repeat the question: often they will make it easier to understand the second time around.

Hypothetical questions

Hypothetical questions make you use your imagination. That may not sound terribly bad, but it means you aren't being allowed to give the interviewer facts, only conjecture. It can often show up a weak interviewer, and yet these questions are all too common. Here are some examples:

♦ 'What do you think you would do if . . . ?'

♦ 'How would you handle a customer who . . . ?'

♦ 'If you had been in charge, how would you have handled it?'

♦ 'Why do you think we put that in the advert?'

To stand out from other candidates, deal with hypothetical questions by treating them as if they were asking for facts anyway. 'Well, when I worked at X I had to do that, and I handled it like this . . .'. This will make you stand out from weak candidates who are speaking from guesswork and imagination, not demonstrating experience and skill.

> Interviewers aren't all fantastic and experienced at asking questions – you may need to help them out, by dealing well with bad questions.

Correcting mistakes

It's not strictly speaking answering questions, but at some stage in an interview, you may well find yourself having to correct a mistake. For example, you may be asked a question which isn't accurate: 'Presumably you've worked with . . . before?' Or, you may be in the interview and suddenly it becomes apparent that the interviewer has got something wrong.

Deal with mistakes immediately

When there is an obvious mistake, deal with it immediately. Letting it go out of politeness may seem the safest option – in the short term, it is. After all, it might be just a slip of the tongue, such as referring to the wrong company or something minor like calling you Mark instead of Mike.

On the other hand, it could be a much more significant mistake – the interviewer may have totally got the wrong idea about something. Letting it go can be dangerous because it may come up again. And the longer you let the interviewer go on believing something and saying it without being corrected, the more confusing it is for the interviewer when you eventually correct him/her.

How to interrupt

If an interviewer makes a mistake, the best way to deal with it is to interrupt him/her. Interrupting is usually a negative behaviour, and something that you should avoid, but in this instance, you need to nip things gently in the bud, and correct any apparent mistake immediately. Here are some tips on how to do it:

♦ Interrupt gently. Interrupting is normally regarded as negative behaviour, so make sure you do it politely.

♦ Apologise for interrupting: 'Sorry, but . . .' People often say that apologising makes you look weak and submissive, but it is perfectly all right to apologise (without making a huge issue of it) if you are interrupting someone – in fact under these circumstances, it's appropriate.

♦ Make eye contact. Look at the interviewer when interrupting him/her – it grabs his/her attention.

♦ Raise your hand slightly, palm towards them. This is a 'stopping signal' in body language, and makes it easier for them to stop and listen to you. It shouldn't be a dramatic gesture like a policeman directing traffic, or like a schoolboy asking teacher

a question – just a slight movement is all that is
necessary.

♦ Point out the interviewer's error politely: 'Sorry,
but it was actually XYZ Ltd, not ABC limited
where I did . . .'.

♦ Smile – it never does any harm!

> Nip misconceptions in the bud before they
> continue. You are building up a picture with the
> interviewer, and you need to make sure it is a
> correct one.

Reinforcing your message

Sometimes you may feel you have not said, or been
given the chance to say, exactly what you wanted to
say. You may want to reinforce your message.

Convincing people by body language

There are certain ways you can convince an interviewer
you are telling the truth:

♦ eye contact – meet their gaze steadily and don't
look away

♦ hand on heart – touch your heart or chest when
making an important point

♦ nod whilst you speak.

Strengthening and emphasising your message

◆ Reinforce your message by repeating it – not too emphatically, just say it then repeat it once.

◆ Reflect back what they say then lead on from there to make your own point. For example: 'I know you've said the job is mainly working on X, so I'd like to make sure you realise just how experienced at this I am.'

Convincing people of the major points you are trying to make can make the difference between an average interview and a performance that will be remembered.

Summary points

◆ **Good questions are easy to answer, so use the time to relax and enjoy yourself! Listen carefully and answer the question.**

◆ **Help the interviewer. Poor questioning technique makes it easy for candidates to give poor answers. Read between the lines and give them the information you think they seek, however badly they phrase the question.**

◆ **Ask for clarification if you need to.**

- ◆ When you need to correct an interviewer's mistakes, be polite but factual. Don't just let it go – it may cause problems later.

- ◆ Be honest and truthful, and use body language to impress on the interviewer that you are doing so where necessary.

Chapter 7

Leave on a Good Note

You'll never make a good first impression on your way out of an interview! But what you can do is blow a good performance by leaving on a low note, or worse, creating a last-minute negative impression.

In this Chapter:

♦ **saying goodbye**
♦ **being remembered**
♦ **final points.**

We have said that the impression people get of you when you first meet them can be lasting and very important. Similarly, when you part you can either reinforce a good impression or ruin all your good work – people do tend to remember the last thing you said or did.

You know the issues about standing up, shaking hands, what to say etc, that we looked at in earlier chapters. Oddly, the relief that you can feel when a stressful interview is over can also affect your behaviour and co-ordination, as your body releases a flood of new hormones and chemicals into your body's bloodstream.

Stay cool and polished until out of sight and earshot of your interviewer – manage your exit in the same way you managed your entrance, and everything will be fine. But you can also use the last few minutes or seconds of your interview to enhance your chances with a good positive sales pitch.

Is this you?

♦ When it's over, I can't wait to get out of there! I can't be bothered with anything but getting away as quickly as possible so I can relax.

♦ I hate that awkward couple of minutes at the end when you're both 'wrapping things up'. I never know what to do.

♦ You can't prepare for the end of an interview – it all depends how well it's gone.

♦ If the first impression counts for so much, why worry about what happens on the way out?

Saying goodbye

The interviewer will usually signal that the interview is at an end.

What to do

♦ Stay seated until the interviewer gets up.

♦ But gather your things together, so there aren't any awkward pauses when you're ready to leave.

- Try to avoid grabbing a hasty last mouthful of water or coffee — it looks rushed and rather odd.

What to say

- Let the interviewer say 'Goodbye' then respond appropriately.

- If he/she doesn't, take the initiative and just say 'Goodbye' politely.

- Compliment them (but not excessively!) by saying, for example: 'It was nice to meet you', or 'It's been a pleasure.'

- Shake hands. If they don't offer their hand, offer yours first.

- Remember what we have said about handshakes. Even if you feel you've done badly, offer a handshake that is confident.

Leaving the room and building

- Keep up your best behaviour until you are out of the interviewer's sight and hearing.

- Remember: you never know who may be around, so be careful to stay professional until you leave the building — you may be on a security camera!

- Lighting a cigarette the second you leave the interviewer's room is sometimes noticed and frowned upon.

- Don't forget to say 'Goodbye . . . and thank you!' to receptionists.

> Interviewers may need help closing the interview
> – many of them find this the most difficult part,
> so you may have to take the initiative!

Being remembered

Prepare good questions

At the end of an interview, you will usually be asked
whether you have any questions. Prepare some in
advance to make sure you always have one or two, as
this helps to make interviewers think you are seriously
interested in the job.

On the other hand, don't go in with a long list – it's
daunting for interviewers and puts them on the spot.
Just think of a maximum of, say, three questions. It's
fine to write them down, but don't make a shopping
list!

Smile and be charming

If you have made any mistakes or if you have been very
serious and professional during the rest of the
interview, this is the time when you can now smile
and appear a little more relaxed. Often, interviewers
who have been nervous will relax at this point too,
so this may be a good chance to find out more
about the company as the atmosphere starts to
relax at last.

You want to leave the impression that you would be a
good part of the organisation's team, so you want to

appear likeable. If you are now asking questions, be especially friendly. The interviewer has been in charge up to this point, asking all the questions. Suddenly, this can be where you get to put him/her on the spot, so be nice about it as he/she can feel under pressure. You want him/her to feel comfortable with you after you have left.

Questions *not* to ask

♦ 'How did I do?' (or any words to that effect). This shows lack of confidence and you may not have done that badly.

♦ 'Is X a problem?' Don't ever highlight problems on the way out. Better by far to hope they have forgotten X (a bad point) and instead highlight Y (your good point) in some way.

♦ 'If I don't get this job can you keep me in mind for anything else?' (or words to that effect!). This just makes you look desperate for work, and it won't do you any favours.

Raise concerns and deal with them

If you think the interviewer has any unstated concerns, or if he/she has expressed any, try to deal with them. For example, an interviewer might say to you that he/she is not sure whether or not your skillset would fit within the team, but that he/she wants to interview several people to see who would be the best fit with their requirements. At the end of the interview, you could address this issue if you felt it would help create or reinforce a positive impression: 'I remember you mentioned the team fit. Can I just say that the team you described is very similar to the one I'm in at present, and I'm sure I could adapt to any differences quickly.'

Obviously, this is a matter for your personal judgement – the golden rule is to finish on a positive note, and to raise nothing negative at the end of your interview.

> When it is your turn to ask questions, don't try to interview the interviewer – he/she won't like it!

Final points

Putting right things that have gone wrong

If anything went badly, such as you being late, or misunderstanding a question completely, bring it up again and put it right if you can. Obviously, if you can't put it right, don't raise it, or you will end on a negative, but where you can, do so: 'I'm so sorry I misinterpreted what you were saying. I hope you'll be able to see now that actually I've got quite a lot of experience at X.'

Having the last word

If you can prepare a few 'parting shots' that are really positive, commit them to memory so you can use whichever seems most appropriate on the day. For example: 'It's been a pleasure to meet you – I've really enjoyed learning more about what you do.'

What *not* to say

- 'I really hope to hear from you.'

- 'Please don't forget to let me know about the outcome.'

- 'Sorry for being late!' (Don't remind them about bad points at this stage)

- 'Good luck with the other interviews!'

- 'I hope you find the right person.' (Remember, you should assume *you* are the right person – that's the image you want to cultivate.)

- 'Thank you for seeing me.'

This is your very, very last chance to make a good impression. Never jeopardise it by saying anything negative.

Summary points

- **Saying a good goodbye is almost as important as making a good greeting. Plan it carefully in advance.**

♦ **Make sure you are remembered by preparing a couple of short 'closers', using the ones that are most appropriate at the time.**

♦ **Always leave on a positive note; never ever leave on a negative note.**

Psychometric Tests for Graduates

Gain the confidence you need to excel at graduate-level psychometric and management tests

Andrea Shavick

This book contains 37 genuine graduate-level practice tests from SHL Group plc, the biggest test publisher in the world; 227 questions covering verbal, numerical, abstract and spatial reasoning, mechanical comprehension, fault diagnosis, accuracy and personality; and genuine practice *Brainstorm*, *Scenarios* and *Fastrack* management tests. Research methods are also covered.

ISBN 978-1-84528-262-2

Practice Psychometric Tests

How to familiarise yourself with genuine recruitment tests and get the job you want

Andrea Shavick

Following the success of Andrea Shavick's *Passing Psychometric Tests* and *Psychometric Tests for Graduates* comes this book, crammed full of even more genuine practice psychometric tests from SHL Group plc, the biggest test publisher in the world. They are the tests used by over 95% of the FTSE 100 companies to select their staff, as do the police, the Civil Service, the Armed Forces . . . the list is endless. So if you're looking for a job, you need this book!

ISBN 978-1-84528-020-8

Management Level Psychometric & Assessment Tests

Everything you need to help you land that senior job
Andrea Shavick

Whether you're after a junior management, senior management or even director level position, or simply want to familiarise yourself with the very latest selection and recruitment techniques this book will meet your needs. It includes:

◆ 35 genuine management levels practice psychometric tests and a guide to online testing.

◆ Everything you need to know about personality questionnaires, plus loads of practice material.

◆ A complete guide to what to expect and how to survive an assessment centre visit.

◆ Detailed information on high-level assessment centre exercises commonly used to test candidates.

◆ A guide to researching your chosen organisation.

ISBN 978-1-84528-028-4

How to be Headhunted

The insider's guide to making executive search work for you
John Purkiss & Barbara Edlmair

If you're looking for a senior executive position – or a seat on the board – this book will tell you what you need to know.

◆ Learn about the search industry and the prominent firms within it

- Understand the recruitment process and make it work to your advantage
- Prepare a persuasive covering letter and a 'head-hunter-friendly' CV

Headhunting has long been shrouded in mystique. This book is *the* insider's guide, packed with practical tips to help you approach executive search firms.

ISBN 978-1-84528-048-2

How To Write a Great CV

Prepare a powerful CV that really works
Paul McGee

This book will help you get your foot in the door – and get that interview. You know you can do the job you're going for, but how do you convince the person you are applying to? What you need is a well-designed CV, and that's where this book will help.

Paul McGee provides insights and tips gained from helping thousands of people from all ages and backgrounds to market themselves successfully.

'This book contains useful specimen CVs, covering letters and case studies, together with sample jobs, action plans and interview preparation tips.' *Office Secretary*

ISBN 978-1-84528-892-7

How To Books are available through all good bookshops, or you can order direct from us through Grantham Book Services.

Tel: +44 (0)1476 541080
Fax: +44 (0)1476 541061
Email: orders@gbs.tbs-ltd.co.uk

Or via our website

www.howtobooks.co.uk

To order via any of these methods please quote the title(s) of the book(s) and your credit card number together with its expiry date.

For further information about our books and catalogue, please contact:

How To Books
Spring Hill House
Spring Hill Road
Begbroke
Oxford OX5 1RX

Visit our web site at

www.howtobooks.co.uk

Or you can contact us by email at info@howtobooks.co.uk